FROM MILLENNIAL TO MILLIONAIRE

A Beginner's Guide for Transforming Your Financial Future

Chase Wrenn

Copyright © Chase Wrenn 2023

All rights reserved. No part of this publication may be reproduced, stored, or transmitted in any form or by any means, electronic, mechanical, photocopying, recording, scanning, or otherwise without written permission from the publisher. It is illegal to copy this book, post it to a website, or distribute it by any other means without permission.

Table of Contents

Foreword

1. Introduction

2. Why Should I Invest?

3. What if I Don't Have Money to Invest?

4. Perspective Shift

5. Budgeting

6. What Is Compound Interest?

7. What Should I Invest In?

8. Dollar-cost Averaging and When to Buy

9. Why Not Just Buy Apple, Google, Amazon, etc.?

10. Should You Hire a Financial Advisor?

11. Where Can I Buy the S&P?

12. Do I need to diversify?

13. Conclusion

References

Foreword

This book aims to educate the younger generation—ages eighteen to thirty-five—about investing for long-term wealth building. Investing can be as advanced as you want it to be or a simplified approach. This method of investing is not for the day trader; it is not sexy and does not produce results overnight. However, the information provided could potentially change how you view money and help transform your financial future. Remember throughout your reading that wealth building is a marathon, not a race. The specific investments mentioned in this book are recommendations only and readers should invest at their own risk. While the term "risk" may cause concern, the investment strategy discussed in this book has a proven track record of over one hundred years of data behind it. It should be noted that this approach does not involve investing in cryptocurrency, real estate, or other high-risk ventures that may yield quick results.

1. Introduction

When we think of how much money we need to retire, we often don't have an answer specific enough to reflect our financial situation. Will Social Security still be around when it comes time for me to retire? How much money is enough? Should I worry about inflation? Setting a specific goal to aim towards on your journey is important. Some might simply state that they want to be rich, or that they want to be a millionaire. Neither of those answers are specific enough to provide confidence that there will be "enough" money accumulated for our retirement. However, what if I told you that you could retire as a multi-millionaire with four million dollars and you don't have to have a degree in finance or earn a six-figure salary to do it? A study from 2021 revealed that the average monthly car payment in America for new vehicles was $648.[6] If you invested $648 each month from ages 25 to 65, and compounded it using the average rate of return of 10.5 percent (explained later), you would have a little over 4.1 million dollars at retirement!

The idea of possessing a million dollars may seem unattainable to some, but I want to assure you that your background, physical attributes, ethnicity, or faith do not determine your financial success. All it takes is setting a specific goal and staying consistent with it to the end. For most, you get used to having a car payment, so why not continue the payment and invest it towards your financial goal once the car has been paid off? Even if you fell short of your goal and only met it halfway, you would still have around two million dollars!

2. Why Should I Invest?

It is never any fun to see your hard-earned dollars disappear. You may view investing as a gamble, and it may feel safer to keep your money in a savings account at your local bank or buried in the backyard in a coffee can like your grandparents did. However, the problem your money now faces is inflation. According to the Bureau of Labor Statistics, in 2022 we saw the highest increase in inflation rates in the last forty years.[9] Inflation rates were as high as 9 percent, meaning that on a million-dollar portfolio, $90,000 was potentially lost to inflation that year. The dollar simply wasn't worth the same as the previous year. Savings accounts do not help combat inflation, as they only offer a small incentive to leave your money parked there. Revisiting the example from the beginning, while the investor has 4.1 million at age 65 if he had put that money into a savings account earning 0.50 percent per year for the same period, he would have around $344,308 by age 65, or about 92 percent less for retirement. This should showcase that **no one has ever gotten rich from saving money**.

"Money Doesn't Buy Happiness."

I despise hearing that money doesn't buy happiness. How happy are you when you have to show up to a job you aren't passionate about, or have to work with that one coworker who you don't quite get along with? How excited are you to work the next few decades until age 67 when the government deems you are at your full retirement age? Having money provides us with the freedom to choose what we want in life. It offers opportunities to travel, explore new restaurants, and even buy our dream home or car. Money gives you the security to leave a job from which you are not getting fulfillment to pursue your passion without the fear of how to make ends meet. Without money, we wouldn't be able to afford medical expenses, gas for our vehicles, or even food to satisfy our hunger. Investing provides us with a means to grow our money without requiring too much of our time. The earlier we can improve our knowledge of how money works, the earlier we can start to multiply it and ultimately leverage our time.

Leveraging your time means getting away from active income as your sole income source. Active income means trading your time to perform a service, also known as the "9 to 5 for a paycheck" philosophy. While you can increase your income by working overtime, this takes precious time away from your family and your personal life. It is also hard to scale—you can only work so much overtime before you cap out or burn out. Simply put, if you aren't physically at work at an active income source, you aren't earning any income. Salary-type jobs are a little better than paid by the hour, but it has limits too. You must wait for annual wage increases or promotions to raise your earning potential and that could take years. It is not until you begin to invest that you can start increasing your wealth passively without having to trade your time for it. I am not talking about active trading, like a day trader. That is a very involved and hands-on way to make money and not ideal for the long term. I like focusing on the investor who buys a fund or a series of funds and automates the monthly contributions. Think about creating a portfolio worth one million dollars that generates a 7 percent return in a year. This portfolio can produce $70,000 in passive income without requiring any physical effort or clocking in. On the other hand, how much overtime and effort would you need to put in to make an additional $70,000 this year? Imagine what you would do with that new free time and how much longer you'd live by not burning yourself out trying to increase your income the hard way. Warren Buffett, one of my favorite investors, has amassed a personal net worth of over one hundred billion dollars. He once famously said, "If you don't find a way to make money while you sleep, you will work until you die." [15] That quote has always stayed with me throughout this wealth-building journey as I learned an investor's biggest asset isn't his income, but more importantly, his *time*. Time can be the difference between needing to invest $500 per month or $1,500 per month to achieve the same financial goal. The earlier you start, the more time you have for your money's compounding effect to take place. In the example from the beginning, an 18-year-old would only have to invest $320 per month to achieve the same 4.1 million at age 65. However, if you waited just 7 years and didn't start until age 25, you would have to save double the amount of $648 each month just to keep up with the 18-year-old! The moral of the story, the earlier you start, the less you will have to consistently put away to reach your goal.

Oftentimes, we come to find out that school has grossly underprepared us for dealing with our finances and handling our money responsibly. Spending money after getting a job and seeing a steady paycheck rolling in is easy, but it is much harder to keep and grow it. Some people don't think about investing for the future until it is too late. It may not be until we find ourselves immersed in massive amounts of student loans, auto loans, and consumer credit card debt that we become aware of our spending habits and begin to seek out answers on how we can get our heads above water.

3. What if I Don't Have Money to Invest?

You may feel like you are currently living paycheck to paycheck and don't have anything extra to get started with an investment strategy. However, most people DO have spare funds to invest after all expenses are paid each month—but that amount varies from person to person based on income and living expenses. The only way to uncover the true amount of money left at the end of the month is through budgeting. For example, Person A might have $1000 left over, while Person B might have only $100. At this point, don't focus too closely on the specific amount because everyone has different needs and financial goals. Additionally, Person A might need to withdraw $100,000 a year in retirement to live comfortably while Person B might only need $25,000. Take time to reflect and assess your financial situation and try to come up with an estimate of how much you would need to live comfortably if you had to retire next year. A popular approach to retirement planning is the "25x" rule which states, "If you plan to maintain your current lifestyle in retirement, making 4 percent withdrawals each year for 30 years, you should save 25 times your current annual expenses in retirement accounts."[3] If we applied the 25x rule to our example, Person A would need 2.5 million to be able to retire and withdraw $100,000 a year, while Person B only needs $625,000 to maintain their lifestyle and withdraw $25,000 per year. Hopefully, this gives you some relief in knowing you might not need as much as you thought saved up to retire.

4. Perspective Shift

One of the best pieces of advice to be successful in this journey—you must change the way you view money. Our relationship with money varies from person to person. Since there is no real formal education geared toward financial discipline, we often mimic our parents and their relationship with money we saw growing up. We may not feel worthy enough to retire as a millionaire, or even believe it is attainable based on where we came from or our family's history with money. You must accept that you are worthy and acknowledge that investing is open to everyone.

In order to change your perspective on money, it is important to identify which category you fall under and understand why you have that particular relationship with money. Some people are savers, and some are spenders. Spenders love having the newest tech products or going shopping and will often say that money burns a hole in their pocket. They enjoy living for the moment and put less thought into financial planning for the future. There is no harm in enjoying your hard-earned dollars and experiencing things. I just know there will come a time when they want to stop working and travel full-time, and that's hard to do if they haven't built up a suitable retirement balance. How easy would the decision be to retire early and travel if you had a few million in the bank? Let me help you get there.

On the opposite side of the spectrum are the savers. Savers are reluctant to spend money and will save at all costs necessary. Think back to the television show with the extreme couponers who go to crazy lengths to save a buck or get something for free. It is not uncommon to see a saver-turned-millionaire still driving a beat-up daily car because it "runs just fine." Individuals who save money so heavily can become accustomed to living frugally, and as they reach retirement age, they may find it difficult to spend their accumulated wealth due to their ingrained habits of saving. It can be mentally challenging for some individuals to spend money even when they have a lot of it. Massive wealth comes when you are able to delay gratification. We all want that nice car or boat right now, however, if you can have patience then your assets can provide those things for you. Notable examples of this are successful icons like Jeff Bezos, who was still driving a Honda Accord when his net worth was around $10 billion, or Warren Buffett still living in the same house today he bought for $31,000 back in 1958. Once you identify which category best describes you, you can then start to take charge of your finances and habits.

5. Budgeting

When it comes to budgeting and monitoring our finances, it is crucial to draw a parallel between money and calories. Losing weight requires a calorie deficit, meaning you must burn more calories than you consume. Conversely, gaining weight requires a calorie surplus. In the realm of budgeting and saving, achieving a surplus of money is only possible if your income exceeds your expenses. It is imperative to keep this in mind if you want to achieve financial stability and security. Simply put, it comes down to "calories in" versus "calories out," or "money in" versus "money out" to meet your financial goals. I won't get too detailed regarding the topic of nutrition, but think of it that way as you assess your budget—calories in versus calories out. Are you in a caloric surplus or a deficit? Please keep in mind that the caloric value of food remains the same whether you are consuming vegetables or ice cream. Despite the difference in quality, 500 calories is still 500 calories. Conversely, whether you spend $50 at the bar during a night out or $50 on gas to commute to work, it is still $50. Despite one being a want and the other being a need, the same logic applies. The key is to budget for known expenses, so they don't surprise you at the end of the month. Some very wealthy couples live paycheck to paycheck even with a $200,000 annual household income. To put it into perspective, a couple making a combined $100,000 could potentially save and invest more than the couple making twice as much if they budgeted correctly. If your budget includes food and drinks out with friends, then there's no harm done. In the same logic—if you save 500 calories from your daily calorie goal and swap it for your favorite dessert, there is no foul there either.

Where's my Money?

People who budget and still don't have surplus funds at the end of the month often end up "nickel and diming" themselves to failure. The $5 here and the $10 there all add up very quickly. These small expenses are similar to a dripping faucet filling up a bucket over time. The drip seems harmless at the beginning just the same as tiny purchases throughout the week. Imagine if you flipped it and threw a little bit each day into a savings jar, it would accumulate just as fast. Oftentimes, you might see someone miss their weight loss goal because they failed to track the calories in things like sodas, condiments, and snacks. Logging the items you eat is the only way to know how many calories you have consumed for the day. Budgeting works the same way, where you track all your expenses so you can know how much money is going out each month and the numbers will never lie (neither will the scale).

      Eating out fast food, grabbing a coffee on the road, buying tobacco products, and subscriptions like Netflix, Hulu, and Amazon Prime all add up the same way calories do. Be honest with yourself—are you overspending? The goal of this chapter is to identify areas in which you could save so you can begin to put those excess dollars into your investment account. Once you determine how much you can invest, you can start paying yourself first. One way to treat yourself is to set aside a fixed amount each month, treating it like a bill payment. Once you've paid that amount, the rest of your funds are available for your personal use. You do not have to give up your daily coffee or kick your nicotine habit. I am simply suggesting that you match your investments for those purchases dollar for dollar. If you spend five dollars per day on a coffee, match yourself five dollars and put that into the investment account. This is a simple reward system that allows you to continue having what you enjoy and not feel guilty about it by maintaining a balance scale. This mental accountability may help you become more aware of your daily purchases. Too much of one or the other can put you out of balance and negatively impact your financial goals.

    You may think to yourself, I don't have an extra $150 dollars to invest each month. However, that five dollars a day for coffee equates to $150 per month, which adds up to $1,800 per year! If you can change your perception of money and become more aware of your spending, you might discover there is more left over than you realize. If I am trying to remain under my caloric intake for the day, I can choose to have ice cream, but I must either burn that same number of calories through exercise or forego another snack for that day to remain under my caloric intake level. Small sacrifices can make a big difference in your budget. Just like skipping a bag of chips to save on calories, you can cut back on unnecessary expenses to stay within your monthly budget.

6. What Is Compound Interest?

I'm not going to spend a ton of time on the subject, but for those who are new to the term ***compound interest*** here is a quick breakdown. Compound interest, as defined by Investopedia, is *"The interest on a loan or deposit calculated based on both the initial principal and the accumulated interest from previous periods."*[19] In simpler terms, it is the interest from your money that makes you more money. Think about standing on top of a mountain and making a snowball. You roll the snowball down the mountain, and it starts to accumulate and grow as it gets further toward the end. Albert Einstein said, "Compound interest is the eighth wonder of the world. He who understands it earns it; he who doesn't pays it."[16] This can be demonstrated by one simple example of compound interest which poses the question, *"Would you rather have a penny that doubles every day for a month or one million Dollars?"* At first glance, it can be easy to choose the million-dollar option over a penny doubling for 30 days. However, what many may fail to realize is just how powerful the compound effect is in this example. The penny doubles every day to ultimately become **$5,368,709.12** on the 30th day.[7] That's five times more money than if you picked the one million dollars initially! To demonstrate just how valuable *time* is in this equation, if you had stopped the compound process early on day 27, and pulled the money out, you would have **$671,088.64.** While this is still impressive and a substantial amount of money, you would be leaving 4.7 million on the table if you pulled it just three days earlier.

Watch what happens to this penny over thirty days!

Day 1	$.01	**Day 16**	$327.68
Day 2	$.02	**Day 17**	$655.36
Day 3	$.04	**Day 18**	$1,310.72
Day 4	$.08	**Day 19**	$2,621.44
Day 5	$.16	**Day 20**	$5,242.88
Day 6	$.32	**Day 21**	$10,485.76
Day 7	$.64	**Day 22**	$20,971.52
Day 8	$1.28	**Day 23**	$41,943.04
Day 9	$2.56	**Day 24**	$83,886.08
Day 10	$5.12	**Day 25**	$167,772.16
Day 11	$10.24	**Day 26**	$335,544.32
Day 12	$20.48	**Day 27**	$671,088.64
Day 13	$40.96	**Day 28**	$1,342,177.28
Day 14	$81.92	**Day 29**	$2,684,354.56
Day 15	$163.84	**Day 30**	$5,368,709.12

This is an extreme example of compounding. Unfortunately, our investments will not double every day as the penny did. Nonetheless, remember this example as you begin planning your wealth-building journey. Know that you are investing for the long term. Once again, wealth building is a marathon and not a race. When you initially start this journey, it is going to seem like it will take forever to build up your account balance. Charlie Munger of Berkshire Hathaway, famous for his one-liners put this into perspective when he said, "The first 100k is a b*tch, but you gotta do it."[17] It takes time, but you will get there. Once you do, the money will start working a little harder for you. It may take you a decade to get to $100,000, but then maybe it only takes 8 years to get to $200,000, then 5 years to get to $300,000, and so on. Look back at the chart of the penny doubling. By Day 12, you have only $20, but as time goes on look at the gap between days 24 and 25. Our compounding investments work similarly, but at a slower pace, and the compound curve begins to take off later down the road. You must stick to the plan no matter what, even when times get tough because you would hate to stop your investment accounts compounding early on Day 27 versus Day 30.

7. What Should I Invest In?

At this point we understand the importance of a budget, we have some money saved, we are familiar with compound interest, and we want to put our money to work. There are countless stocks and funds out there and it can be very intimidating to try and think about what to invest in.

Instead of trying to pick the right stock or what could potentially become the next Amazon, I recommend investing in the S&P 500. The S&P 500 Index, or Standard & Poor's 500 Index, is a market-capitalization-weighted index of five hundred leading publicly traded companies in the United States.[2] Investing in the S&P 500 is a solid long-term choice with ample evidence backing its success. You might recognize some big company names within this group such as Apple, Amazon, Tesla, and Google. These companies along with a vast list of others make up the S&P 500. The S&P has returned on average around 10.5 percent since its inception date back in 1957.[12] Shorter time frames reveal a ten-year annual return of 14 -17 percent, but in long-term wealth building, we want to zoom out and focus on the lifetime return or "since inception performance." Yes, there have been some bad years like 2008-2009 when it lost 46 percent, but over time it has won. Although we have experienced several major economic downturns like the Dot-com bubble, the financial crisis of 2008, and most recently the COVID-19 pandemic, the market (S&P) has always recovered and will continue to thrive.

A lot of today's millionaires were made from consistent investing through these market downturns. Looking back at the bottom of the market following the crash of 2008 to November 2021, the S&P 500 was up over 400 percent for the investors who stuck through the hard times and continued to buy. There have been several instances of overall stock market decline, including the recent COVID-19 pandemic. However, if you examine the low in March 2020 up until January 2023, you will see that the market has still increased by 65 percent. Moreover, it has gone up by almost 39 percent in the last five years.

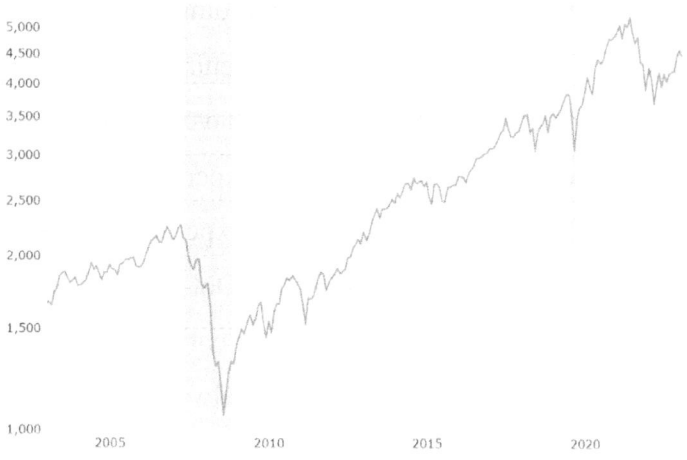

The S&P occasionally experiences significant declines, which presents an opportunity for new investors to purchase S&P stocks at a discounted price. If you are kicking yourself for not starting to invest earlier, you are getting a rare opportunity to buy in at the same price others were paying a few years ago. Think about the price of fuel. If gas was $3 a gallon on Monday and fell 50 percent to $1.50 per gallon by Friday, would you be happy or avoid buying it altogether? Why should buying stocks be any different when they are down in value? While others are panicking and selling, that is the time for us to buy and increase our holdings while they are discounted.

The worst thing you can do on your wealth-building journey is to listen to broke friends and family and panic sell your stocks. Panic sales can be explained in a simple metaphor. If you paid $40,000 for a new vehicle and a year later someone offered you $20,000 and told you that's all it was worth, would you sell it? Hopefully, the answer would be no. You know and understand it is worth more than that and would regret selling your new vehicle to someone for half of what you paid for it. Stocks operate the exact same way. The only time you truly lose on a stock is when you sell it at a lower price than what you bought it. In the car example, because you know what it was worth when you bought it, you sold it to the lowest bidder and just realized a $20,000 loss. Logically, you should keep your vehicle knowing its worth and simply ignore the lowball offer. It is no different when a stock is valued at $100 per share when you buy it and then falls to $50 per share. You should simply keep it rather than give it away to the lowest bidder. In the world of investing sometimes it is simply a battle of buyers versus sellers. **To make money, someone must lose money.**

8. Dollar-cost Averaging and When to Buy

As with diets and weight loss, the greatest recipe for success in long-term investing is consistency. Setting aside a monthly allotment for investments and having that on an automatic schedule will ensure you don't forget or neglect to contribute each month. The notion of thinking you can time the market and buy when prices are down is a lost cause. You can run a multitude of scenarios where person A invests consistently and person B tries to time the market. Person A will always have a higher ending balance. This is due to dollar-cost averaging (DCA). In a nutshell, this means you are buying consistently on a fixed basis which results in buying when the market is up, down, and trading sideways, changing your average cost over time. This is beneficial when the market is down and you are buying at discounted rates, compared to Person B who might be waiting for the bottom that never comes. There are still investors waiting for a certain stock to get below a price before they buy it, and it may never drop back down that low. If you were to pull up any decent stock's performance chart, you would see that every 52-week high eventually becomes its 52-week low if the stock continues to rise over time. No matter what the market is doing, maintain consistency with your buying.

The same is true with diet and exercise, would you agree that one workout or eating one healthy meal won't help you reach your fitness goals? I always liked the metaphor of planting an Appleseed with the hopes of growing an apple tree that produces fruit. Would you plant the seed, water it a few times, and then dig it up to see the progress? Growing a tree (or a large portfolio) takes time and consistent rain, and sunshine. The tree might take 30 years to grow, but once it begins to produce fruit, that could feed you for a lifetime (equivalent to dividends for income in retirement).

9. Why Not Just Buy Apple, Google, Amazon, etc.?

So why is the S&P 500 the superior investment as opposed to investing in a single stock or company? Let's answer that by relating it to the game of Roulette. Roulette is a gambling game consisting of numbers 0, 00 (green), and 1-36 in the colors red or black.

There's no denying that if you placed your bet on a single number and won, the payout is exponential. How often does that happen? The odds are 35 to 1—or about a 3 percent chance of winning. If you relate that to investing, you could say you might pick 35 bad investments before you pick the right one. There is also a betting strategy of picking either red or black, which gives you closer to a 50 percent chance of winning unless you hit zero and double zero, which leaves you with nothing. While this equates to a 50 percent chance of winning, if you have ever played Roulette, you know how easily your money can disappear using this betting strategy. Betting on red or black pays out 1 to 1 while betting specific numbers payout 35 to 1. In the gambling world, the bigger the risk, the bigger the reward. The same can be said for investing. You might get lucky with a cryptocurrency or penny stock that skyrocketed from a few cents to a few dollars, but that doesn't happen often. It is also proven that the longer you sit and play, the better chance the house (casino) has of winning. When you relate this to stocks, your big gain might be wiped out by a series of poor investments. That means that the people who got lucky a few times with a penny stock have a high chance of losing it all if they continue to play those risky investments.

What if there was a bet you could make so that no matter which number or color the ball landed on you had a 70-80 percent chance of winning? Historical data shows the S&P has gained value in 40 out of the last 50 years, which equates to an 80 percent win rate. Remember, there must be some level of risk in investing for you to make money. Forget the green zeros for a second and consider that if you placed one dollar on red and one dollar on black, you would never make any money because there is no risk. The payout comes from choosing one color and risking your dollar to the fates of where the ball lands, similar to flipping a quarter and calling heads or tails.

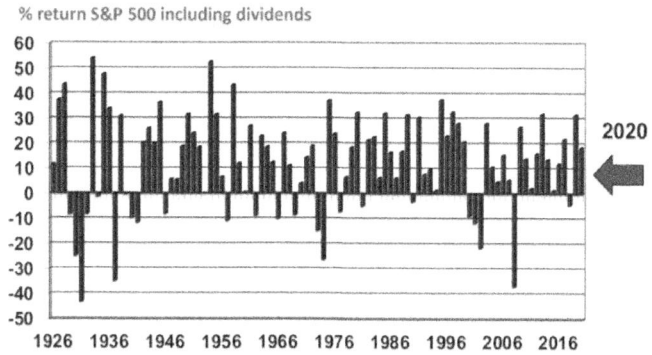

The S&P has made investors money 80 percent of the time. This should relax your fear of losing money when investing in the S&P a little. Even if one company has a horrible year, another one might be having its best year and this balance offsets any major losses to the investor. Investing in a single company or stock could yield a huge return if that stock is successful in the future, but it could also wipe out your investment gains just as quickly as betting on the wrong number. In long-term investing, you don't want to have to worry about one bad bet wiping you out, so it is best to spread your money out on all the numbers in the game so you get a piece of the action no matter what hits. If you get nothing out of this book then at least you will have a general understanding of Roulette next time you are in a casino!

10. Should You Hire a Financial Advisor?

My aim in this section is not to sway you one way or the other, but rather to provide you with the necessary information to make an informed decision on your own about whether you should hire a financial advisor to manage your assets. Financial advisor's fees can vary, the industry average consensus is usually to charge 1 percent of Assets under Management (AUM). The downside to this is that they will charge you this fee even if the stock market is down that year and you have negative returns. There can also be hourly-based fees for consultations and planning that reach up to $400 per hour.

While a financial advisor might work for some, it is important to note that financial advisors don't always offer the best results. In fact, a study from 2021 revealed that 94 percent of investment professionals underperformed in the market and couldn't beat the S&P's returns.[4] That meant that only 6 percent of hired advisors beat the market. Depending on fees, this would determine how much of that positive return was left to stay in the client's pocket.

Back in 2007, Warren Buffett placed a million-dollar bet that after all fees and expenses, a boring low-cost index fund mirroring the S&P 500 would outperform a hand-picked portfolio of hedge funds over ten years. Buffett won his bet against a hedge fund that accepted his challenge, proving that even with all the manpower and resources, hedge funds couldn't consistently outperform the market. The hedge funds had an average annual return of 2.2 percent, while Buffet's index fund averaged 7.1 percent.[13] Knowing they couldn't catch up, the hedge fund conceded early in the bet and admitted defeat before the time was up. This was a massive win for the average investor because it proved that you didn't need to be part of an exclusive hedge fund to make money. Buffet proved that the average person could buy a low-cost index fund and succeed in the game of investing.

To wrap up the discussion on fees, remember that while compound interest is amazing, you can't forget that fees compound as well. Several studies have been completed on fees and how they negatively affect your retirement balance. One study completed by Forbes imagined a scenario of investing $1000 a month over 40 years earning 9.7 percent. The ending balance was around 4.3 million, another great example of the power of compound interest! However, the 1 percent fee cost the investor about 1.5 million, meaning around 25 percent of their wealth was lost to fees.[1] Another study by NerdWallet showed the hefty impact of fees on a sample portfolio with $25,000 invested initially, contributing $10,000 every year, and earning a 7 percent annual return. They paid 1 percent in fees, and at the end of the 40 years they had sacrificed more than $590,000 to fees![14] Both studies revealed around 25 percent of the investor's portfolio was lost if they paid 1 percent over the long term in fees. In Tony Robbin's book *Money: Master the Game,* he shared from his extensive research that the average cost of owning a mutual fund was 3.17 percent per year.[8] You may be thinking, "Three percent doesn't sound too bad." Well, it is important to note that the cheapest index fund can cost as little as 0.015 percent annually, or $1.50 for every $10,000 invested per year. Now that you know the impact that 1 percent in fees can have on your portfolio over time, imagine tripling it to 3 percent.

So, if you're looking for a hands-off approach to managing your finances, a financial advisor can provide peace of mind. In downturns of the market, they can provide knowledge and expertise to keep you grounded—and that is something on which you really can't put a price. If you are busy and don't have the time or desire to handle financial matters, a professional can take care of it for you. To be clear, I am not against financial advisors; I am one myself and I have a passion for helping others achieve their goals. Unfortunately, they cannot do their job for free no matter how rewarding it is. My goal is to offer valuable information to users so that they can make well-informed decisions based on their individual circumstances.

11. Where Can I Buy the S&P?

While you can't invest directly in the S&P 500, you can buy low-cost index funds and exchange-traded funds (ETFs) that track and mirror their performance. Some of the most popular and my personal favorites include Vanguard's **VFIAX** (what Buffett used to win his bet), **VOO** (ETF), and the Fidelity fund **FXAIX**. These funds have some of the lowest expense ratios in their sector and track the performance of the S&P 500. When you self-manage your accounts, you can ensure you are keeping your costs low to maximize the compound effect. An example of the performance of VFIAX is shown below with $10,000 invested with no additional contributions and it grows to around $44,000 in just ten years![11] The example of VFIAX below has an expense ratio of 0.04 percent, meaning it costs $4 per every $10,000 invested to own per year. In a million-dollar portfolio, it will cost you $400 dollars to own that single fund and self-manage your account versus potentially paying an advisor a $10,000 (1 percent AUM) fee.

Vanguard 500 Index Admiral VFIAX ★★★★★

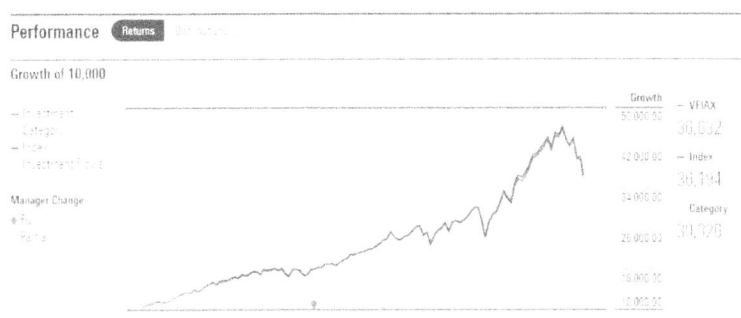

There are a few ways to buy ownership into the S&P. An S&P investment will be classified as an "index fund" and be categorized as either a mutual fund or an exchange-traded fund (ETF). These investments are different in how they operate, trade, and how much they cost to own. It is important to know a few key differences as you decide which is right for you. Here is a basic breakdown of each:

- **Mutual Fund:** They are actively managed and charge an expense ratio to pay for this service—think of it as a salary for the team running and managing it. They trade outside of normal market hours, unlike stocks. They are good for buying fractional shares, which is helpful for the DCA strategy. For example, if a mutual fund costs $75 per share and I contribute $100 each month, I will buy 1.25 shares. They typically will generate a higher return, but bear in mind the fees to own it are usually higher.

- **ETF:** They are passively managed which keeps fees low. They trade like stocks during normal market hours, so they can be sold short and usually trade in whole shares. So, if the same ETF is $75, my $100 contribution would only buy one share. This is generally how they operate; however, some brokers do offer fractional ETF shares.

There are numerous S&P index funds that are not included in my list. Several brokers provide their version of an S&P fund, and if you serve in the military or work for the government and participate in the Thrift Savings Plan, you can purchase the S&P by selecting the C Fund.

12. Do I need to diversify?

You may have heard the age-old saying, "Don't put all your eggs in one basket." This is true because it can be extremely risky to own a single stock due to the volatile nature of a company, just like betting all your money on your favorite number in roulette. The possibility of massive swings in either direction could take years to recover any money lost. If you were to ask me how many stocks I own and I told you 300, would you feel I was diversified enough? The answer is probably yes, however, what if those 300 were condensed into 1 ETF? Owning an index fund that tracks the S&P makes your portfolio diversified. For instance, VFIAX holds 508 different stocks in one fund, while VTSAX has 3,963 stocks in its total market fund. This shows how large these funds can become. If one stock has a bad year, another one's success helps to offset its losses. As a company falls out, it is replaced by another that will benefit the fund. A list came out back in 2007 stating that only 86 of the original 500 companies from 1957 were still in the S&P, showing it is a revolving door bringing in the best and getting rid of stocks that aren't keeping up with the standard.[9] This should give you confidence that the S&P isn't some outdated investment our parents used to make and that it is relevant and suitable for today's investors.

What Type of Account Do I Need?

There are a ton of different brokers and brokerage houses out there including Vanguard, Fidelity, Charles Schwab, TD Ameritrade, and the list goes on. Each of these offers various accounts from which you can choose. To keep it simple, I am going to share the three main accounts and give a basic overview of each to get you started on your wealth-building journey.

The **individual taxable brokerage account** is a non-retirement account where you buy funds with your after-tax dollars. There is no early withdrawal penalty and no annual contribution limit on how much you can put in there. Taxes are easy since you contribute after-tax dollars in there, the only taxes incurred would be on the gains it produces. For example, if I put $100,000 into a fund and a year later it has grown to $110,000, I can cash it all out and will only be taxed on the $10,000 gain. I can also let it grow and compound for the rest of my life and pull from it in retirement by paying income taxes on the money withdrawn each year.

The next and my favorite of the three we will discuss is the **Roth IRA** (Individual Retirement Account). This account is for retirement as depicted by the name and offers the best tax advantages. This is because you contribute after-tax dollars once again, but here's the best part—at retirement, all the gains are tax-free. Unlike the individual taxable account, there is an annual limit to how much you can contribute each year, for 2023 it was $6,500 or $7,500 if you were over the age of 50.[18] So, what's so special about a Roth? Well, let's pretend tax rates in 30 years are 50 percent flat across the board and you have a million bucks in your Roth IRA. Every penny of that is tax-free and stays in your pocket. There is a 10 percent penalty if you try and withdraw from it before age 59.5. However, there are certain circumstances where you can avoid this penalty, such as pulling $10,000 for a first-time home purchase, or you have become permanently disabled after owning it for five years. Again, this is a very basic overview of Roth IRAs and how they operate. If you are 18 to 40 years old, I highly recommend you choose a Roth IRA and max it out each year, even if you already have a 401k or employer-sponsored plan. You can let a Roth compound for the rest of your life and continue to contribute to it if you still have earned income. There are income limits established by the IRS on who can participate in a Roth but don't get discouraged as there are ways around this known as a "Backdoor Roth" for high-wage earners.

Lastly, I wanted to mention the **Traditional IRA**. This, like the Roth, is another retirement account. You cannot touch it until you're at least 59.5 years old, or there will be a 10 percent early withdrawal penalty. The difference between the two comes down to tax treatment. Traditional IRA contributions are tax-deferred, meaning if you max out the annual contribution limit (same limits as Roth) then you will receive a tax reduction for that year. The Traditional IRA can grow tax-deferred until you reach age 72-73 when you must then take a Required Minimum Distribution (RMD) from your Traditional and 401k accounts.[18] Uncle Sam has allowed your money to grow tax-deferred your whole life and now they are saying, "We need our cut and will force you to take an RMD." Failure to pull your RMD will result in a 50 percent excise tax, or a government-imposed tax, on that amount. Thankfully, there are calculators out there to tell you exactly how much you need to withdraw each year to avoid that.

There is much more information out there on IRAs and the differences between the two, but this should help get you to think about which one is right for you. Keep in mind that with the Traditional and Roth IRAs, you cannot open and max out both. If you are under the age of 50, the annual limit you can contribute to an IRA for 2023 was $6,500, so you could technically put $3,250 in a Roth and $3,250 in a Traditional. Your investment is legal and appropriate as long as you don't exceed the IRS contribution limit. To use an extreme example to summarize this, you could technically open 6,500 different IRA accounts and put one dollar in each.

13. Conclusion

I hope that by now you have learned some new concepts and feel more confident when it comes to investing and what to invest in. It is important to keep in mind that time is your most valuable asset when it comes to achieving your goals. Therefore, within 24 hours of reading this book, I recommend that you take action and establish an investment account or an IRA if you do not already have one. Since this is a beginner's guide, I challenge you to continue to seek out information and improve your financial literacy. Even though I have outlined a simple process for investing to build wealth in this book, most people will still hesitate and feel they aren't ready to invest. Or they will ignore the tried-and-true strategies because we as humans often desire to become rich overnight. We may take unnecessary risks by buying stocks on the advice of our friends and coworkers, and we can be very impatient. This can lead to losing money and setting you back significantly in your financial goals. Remember that there will be dips and bad days in the stock market, but you must remain steady and look out 30 years from now. Will a few bad days, weeks, or even months matter in the long run when you have accumulated over a million dollars? Stay hungry, always seek knowledge, and best of luck on your journey toward building wealth.

About the Author

Chase Wrenn has achieved a long-standing goal by writing his debut book, From Millennial to Millionaire, showcasing an effective method for building wealth. Chase was born in Durham, North Carolina, and is a Marine Corps veteran. He has always had a passion for finance and teaching others how to achieve financial independence. He also earned the Accredited Asset Management Specialist (AAMS™) designation from the College for Financial Planning to assist individuals in managing and increasing their wealth.

References

1. Berger, R. (2021, February 5). *How a 1% investment fee can wreck your retirement*. Forbes. Retrieved June 29, 2022, from https://www.forbes.com/sites/robertberger/2021/02/05/how-a-1-investment-fee-can-wreck-your-retirement/?sh=9fbb664611a5
2. Kenton, W. (2023, June 21). *S&P 500 index: What it's for and why it's important in investing*. Investopedia. https://www.investopedia.com/terms/s/sp500.asp
3. Irby, L. T. (2021, November 4). *The multiply-by-25 rule for retirement saving*. The Balance. Retrieved March 1, 2023, from https://www.thebalancemoney.com/multiply-by-twenty-five-rule-retirement-saving-5101329
4. Liu, B., & Sinha, G. (2022, May 9). *Over a recent 20-year period, what percent of professionals investing in large companies "beat the market?"*. Qod: Over the recent 20yr period, what % of investing pros beat the MKT? - blog. Retrieved June 23, 2022, from https://www.ngpf.org/blog/question-of-the-day/question-of-the-day-over-a-recent-20-year-period-what-percent-of-pros-investing-in-large-companies-beat-the-market/
5. *Morningstar, inc.*. Morningstar. (n.d.). Retrieved June 23, 2022, from

https://www.morningstar.com/funds/xnas/vfiax/performance

6. Meyer, S. (2022). *Average new car payment hits $648: How to calculate and lower monthly.* Retrieved February 14, 2023, from https://www.thezebra.com/resources/driving/average-car-payment-2022/

7. *A penny doubled for 30 days is how much?* TraderLion. (2023, February 8). Retrieved February 14, 2023, from https://traderlion.com/quick-reads/penny-doubled-for-30-days/

8. Robbins, Tony (2017). *Money: Master the game.* Simon & Schuster Ltd.

9. *S&P releases list of 86 companies in the S&P 500 since 1957.* Global Paper Money. (2007, March 5). Retrieved February 15, 2023, from https://www.globalpapermoney.com/s-p-releases-list-of-86-companies-in-the-s-p-500-since-1957-cms-1023

10. U.S. Bureau of Labor Statistics. (2022, July 18). *Consumer prices up 9.1 percent over the year ended June 2022, largest increase in 40 years.* U.S. Bureau of Labor Statistics. Retrieved February 23, 2023, from https://www.bls.gov/opub/ted/2022/consumer-prices-up-9-1-percent-over-the-year-ended-june-2022-largest-increase-in-40-years.htm

11. *Vanguard 500 index admiral Vfiax performance.* Morningstar, Inc. (n.d.). Retrieved February 14, 2023, from

https://www.morningstar.com/funds/xnas/vfiax/performance

12. Vernon, S. (2021, January 14). *S&P 500's impressive rate-of-return score: 70-25*. Forbes. Retrieved March 2, 2023, fromhttps://www.forbes.com/sites/stevevernon/2021/01/14/sp-500s-impressive-rate-of-return-score-70-25/?sh=5c46a93ea102

13. Wiles, R. (2018, March 7). *Warren Buffett made a 10-year bet on his market strategy. here's how he won*. USA Today. Retrieved February 28, 2023, from https://www.usatoday.com/story/money/markets/2018/03/07/warren-buffett-made-10-year-bet-his-market-strategy-heres-how-he-won/402823002/

14. Yochim, D., & Todd, J. (2016, April 27). *How a 1% fee could cost millennials $590,000 in retirement savings*. NerdWallet. Retrieved June 29, 2022, from https://www.nerdwallet.com/blog/investing/millennial-retirement-fees-one-percent-half-million-savings-impact/

15. Raisinghani, V. (2023, August 3). Warren Buffett warns that you will "work until you die" if you can't find a way to make money while you sleep . Yahoo! Finance. https://finance.yahoo.com/news/warren-buffett-warns-until-die-113000300.html

16. Einstein's 8th Wonder of the World. CLEARWEALTH Asset Management. (2017, April 28). https://www.clearwealthasset.com/einsteins-8th-wonder-of-the-world/

17. Clark, C. (2023, May 13). "it's a B----, but you gotta do it": Charlie Munger says that your first $100k is the toughest to earn - but most crucial for building wealth here's why it's such a magical milestone. Yahoo! Finance. https://finance.yahoo.com/news/b-gotta-charlie-munger-says-140000516.html
18. Powers, S. (2023, February 26). 9 things you may not know about your ira. Investopedia. https://www.investopedia.com/articles/retirement/08/11-things-to-know-iras.asp
19. Fernando, J. (2023, May 18). The power of compound interest: Calculations and examples. Investopedia. https://www.investopedia.com/terms/c/compoundinterest.asp

Made in United States
North Haven, CT
16 September 2023